# RELIGIONS AROUND THE WORLD

# Islam

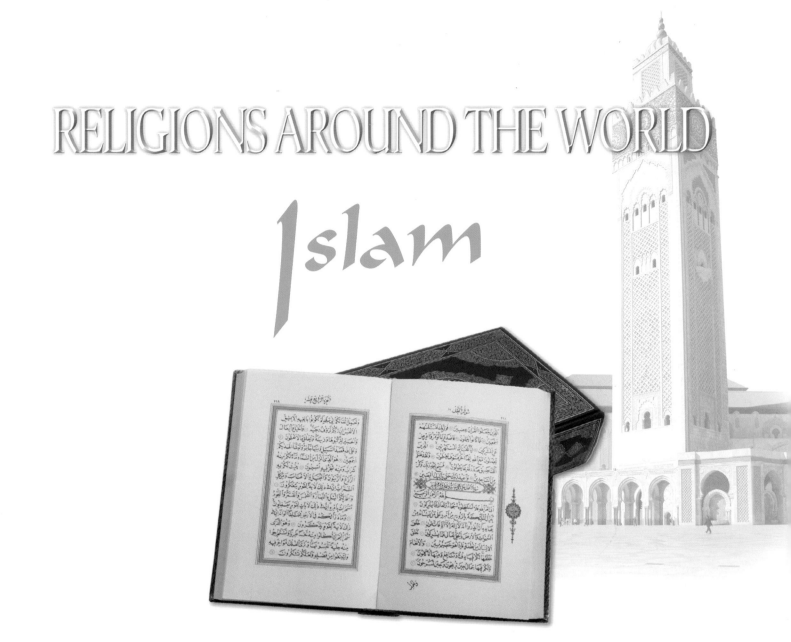

## Katy Gerner

Marshall Cavendish
Benchmark

New York

This edition first published in 2009 in the United States of America by Marshall Cavendish Benchmark.

Marshall Cavendish Benchmark
99 White Plains Road
Tarrytown, NY 10591
www.marshallcavendish.us

First published in 2008 by
MACMILLAN EDUCATION AUSTRALIA PTY LTD
15–19 Claremont Street, South Yarra 3141

Visit our website at www.macmillan.com.au or go directly to www.macmillanlibrary.com.au

Associated companies and representatives throughout the world.

Copyright © Katy Gerner 2008

Library of Congress Cataloging-in-Publication Data

Gerner, Katy.
    Islam / by Katy Gerner.
        p. cm. — (Religions around the world)
    Includes index.
    ISBN 978-0-7614-3167-1
    1. Islam—Juvenile literature.  I. Title.
    BP161.3.G47 2008
297—dc22
                                    2008002849

Edited by Erin Richards
Text and cover design by Cristina Neri, Canary Graphic Design
Photo research by Legend Images
Illustration on p. 14 by Andy Craig and Nives Porcellato
Map courtesy of Geo Atlas; modified by Raul Diche

Printed in the United States

**Acknowledgments**

The author would like to thank Sheikh Khalil Chami and Kawkab Jeda for their suggestions, their wisdom and their time spent reviewing this book.

The author and the publisher are grateful to the following for permission to reproduce copyright material:

Front cover photograph (main): Boys study the Koran in a madrasa, Libya © Charles O. Cecil/Alamy/Photolibrary. Other images: book background © Felix Möckel/iStockphoto; Koran © Kenneth C. Zirkel/iStockphoto; mosque in Singapore © En Tien Ou/iStockphoto; mosque in Casablanca © narvikk/iStockphoto; mosque in Kazakhstan © Igor Zhorov/iStockphoto; Star and Crescent based on image by Tamer Yazici/Shutterstock.

Photos courtesy of: © Shafia Hussaini/123RF, 12 (right); AAP Image/AP Photo/Muchtar Zakaria, 11 (bottom); AAP Image/James Pevitt, 21 (top); © Charles O. Cecil/Alamy, 25 (bottom); Arif Ali/AFP/Getty Images, 17 (bottom); Odd Andersen/AFP/Getty Images, 9 (bottom); Rob Elliott/AFP/Getty Images, 23; Sajjad Hussain/AFP/Getty Images, 7; Peter Parks/AFP/Getty Images, 16 (top); Islamic School/The Bridgeman Art Library/Getty Images, 15; Muhannad Fala'ah/Getty Images, 29 (bottom); Per-Anders Pettersson/Getty Images, 26 (bottom); Reza/Getty Images, 13 (top); Jon Spaull/Getty Images, 8 (bottom); Amy Toensing/Getty Images, 24; © Alija/iStockphoto, 5 (bottom); © vera bogaerts/iStockphoto, 20 (main); © Karim Hesham/iStockphoto, 3 (bottom); © Aman Khan/iStockphoto, 4 (bottom center left), 30 (top right); © Klaas Lingbeek-van Kranen/iStockphoto, 20 (top inset); © Vasko Miokovic/iStockphoto, 4 (center); © murat Şen/iStockphoto, 6 (top); © Owusu-Ansah/iStockphoto, 4 (bottom center right); © Richard Stamper/iStockphoto, 4 (bottom right); © Bob Thomas/iStockphoto, 4 (bottom left); © Igor Zhorov/iStockphoto, 6 (bottom); © Kenneth C. Zirkel/iStockphoto, 1 (left), 5 (top); NASA Goddard Space Flight Center, 4 (center behind); Brynn Bruijn/Saudi Aramco World/PADIA, 28; Katrina Thomas/Saudi Aramco World/PADIA, 22 (top); Nik Wheeler/Saudi Aramco World/PADIA, 27; © wael hamdan/Shutterstock, 10 (top); © Timothy Lee Lantgen/Shutterstock, 19 (bottom); © Gordon Swanson/Shutterstock, 4 (top); USAID/Thomas Hartwell, 18 (bottom); Wikimedia Commons, Public Domain, 9 (top), 19 (top right, center right).

Photos used in book design: book background © Felix Möckel/iStockphoto, 10, 11, 22, 25; mosque in Casablanca © narvikk/iStockphoto, 1, 16, 24, 27, 31; mosque in Kazakhstan © Igor Zhorov/iStockphoto, 3, 18, 22, 26, 32; mosque in Singapore © En Tien Ou/iStockphoto, 8, 18, 22–23, 25, 29, 30; parchment background © Andrey Zyk/iStockphoto, 12, 13, 18, 19; Star and Crescent based on image by Tamer Yazici/Shutterstock, 3, 5, 17, 31.

While every care has been taken to trace and acknowledge copyright, the publisher tenders their apologies for any accidental infringement where copyright has proved untraceable. Where the attempt has been unsuccessful, the publisher welcomes information that would redress the situation.

*For Kym, Lucy, Brendan and Sean*

1 3 5 6 4 2

# Contents

## Glossary words

When a word is printed in **bold**, you can look up its meaning in the Glossary on page 31.

# World Religions

Religion is a belief in a supernatural power that must be loved, worshipped, and obeyed. A world religion is a religion that is practiced throughout the world. The five core world religions are Christianity, Islam, Hinduism, Buddhism and Judaism.

People practicing a religion follow practices that they believe are pleasing to their god or gods. Followers read sacred **scriptures** and may worship either privately at home or in a place of worship. They often carry out special rituals, such as when a baby is born, a couple gets married, or someone dies. Religious people have beliefs about how they should behave in this life, and also about life after death.

Learning about world religions can help us to understand each other's differences. We learn about the different ways people try to lead good lives and make the world a better place.

World religions are practiced by many people of different cultures.

# Islam

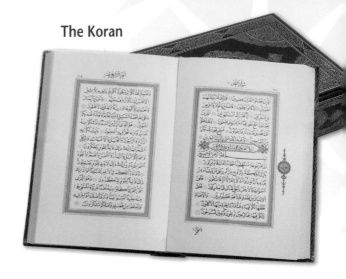

Islam is the religion of Muslims. *Islam* means *peace through willing submission to Allah*. The word *Muslim* means *one who **submits** to Allah*. Allah is the Muslim name for God.

Muslims believe that there is one god, Allah, and that Mohammad is his messenger. The Muslim scripture is called the Koran, or Qur'an. The Koran shows Muslims how Allah wants them to live. Islam influences every aspect of Muslim life, including:

☪ worship practices

☪ family life

☪ eating habits

☪ the way they wash and dress.

Muslims believe in the prophets discussed in the Jewish scriptures. They believe in Jesus but, unlike Christians, they believe Jesus was a prophet and not the Son of God.

There are two main branches of Islam:

☪ the Sunnis, who make up about 84 to 90 percent of the world's Muslims

☪ the Shi'ites.

The Sunnis and Shi'ites practice Islam in a similar way but have different beliefs about who were Mohammad's **successors**.

**The crescent and star form the universal symbol of Islam.**

The Sajdah prayer position, with the forehead touching the ground, symbolizes willing submission to Allah.

# Religious Beliefs

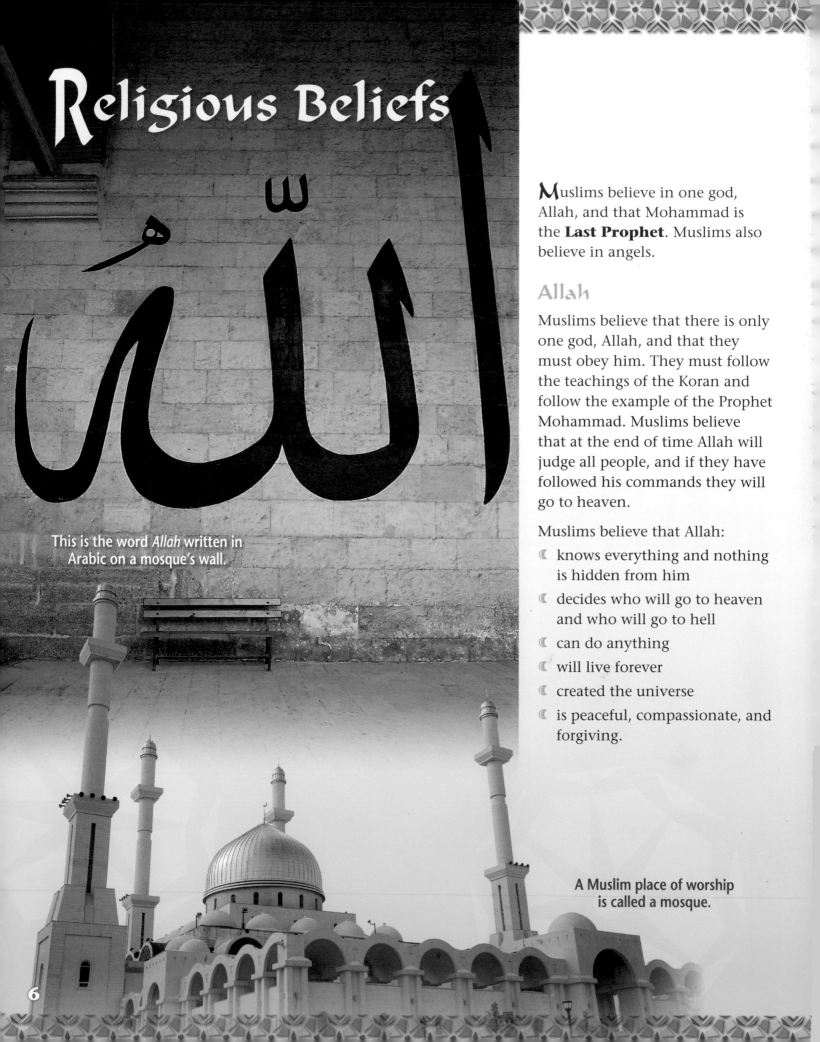

الله

This is the word *Allah* written in Arabic on a mosque's wall.

Muslims believe in one god, Allah, and that Mohammad is the **Last Prophet**. Muslims also believe in angels.

## Allah

Muslims believe that there is only one god, Allah, and that they must obey him. They must follow the teachings of the Koran and follow the example of the Prophet Mohammad. Muslims believe that at the end of time Allah will judge all people, and if they have followed his commands they will go to heaven.

Muslims believe that Allah:

☾ knows everything and nothing is hidden from him

☾ decides who will go to heaven and who will go to hell

☾ can do anything

☾ will live forever

☾ created the universe

☾ is peaceful, compassionate, and forgiving.

A Muslim place of worship is called a mosque.

Muslims study the Koran, which contains the teachings of the Last Prophet.

## The Last Prophet

Muslims believe that Mohammad, who lived in the seventh century CE, is the Last Prophet. They believe that Mohammad received messages from Allah during his life. These teachings make up the Koran.

It is considered disrespectful to draw pictures or show images of Mohammad. A movie made of his life used an actor who portrayed him off-camera.

Muslims always add the words "Sallallahu alaihi wa sallam" after they say the Prophet's name. It means "the peace and blessings of Allah be upon him."

## Angels

Muslims believe that Allah created angels from light. These angels can change their appearance and they also have a number of duties. These are:

☾ to praise Allah

☾ to carry Allah's throne

☾ to carry his message.

Muslims believe everyone has two guardian angels who are always with them to guide and help them. Angels write down the good and bad deeds of each person in a book. Allah will use this book at the end of time when he judges everybody.

# Beliefs About Behavior

All Muslims must observe the Five Pillars of Islam and must behave truthfully, generously, and respectfully. Some Muslims also serve Allah as muftis, imams, or sheiks.

## The Five Pillars of Islam

The Five Pillars of Islam, which Muslims must follow, are:

☾ reciting the shahadah, which is "there is no god but Allah and his Prophet is Mohammad"

☾ praying five times a day

☾ **fasting** from dawn to sunset during **Ramadan**

☾ giving to charity

☾ going on a **pilgrimage** to **Mecca** at least once in their lifetime (if they can afford it).

## Truthfulness, Generosity, and Respect

Muslims must be truthful, generous, and respectful in their everyday lives. They must:

☾ tell the truth

☾ deal fairly with other people

☾ avoid killing anybody

☾ avoid doing evil

☾ teach other people about the Koran

☾ not make pictures of Allah or Mohammad

☾ not quarrel over money or anything else

☾ not charge interest on loans or deal with interest

☾ give two-fifths of their income to charity.

The practice of praying five times a day is called salat and is one of the Five Pillars of Islam.

## Muftis, Imams, and Sheiks

Muftis, imams, and sheiks are very important leaders in Muslim communities. They are responsible for guiding their communities so they follow Mohammad's teachings. Sometimes, they become politicians to encourage a wider audience to follow the Prophet's teachings. They are expected to provide spiritual guidance in their duties as a politician.

### Muftis

Muftis are highly trained Islamic scholars, responsible for interpreting Islamic law. Their duties include giving legal opinions on issues, either privately or to judges. These legal opinions are called fatwas.

### Imams

Imams are leaders of Islamic **congregations**. They lead the prayers and preach **sermons** in mosques.

### Sheiks

Traditionally, "sheik" is the word for a tribal leader and means "elder" or "revered wise man." Sheiks are elected by the community. They solve disputes, such as arguments between a husband and wife or who owns a particular piece of land. Sheiks are also responsible for the poorer members of the community. A sheik's wife is considered very important and receives much respect from the community.

These days, a sheik can also perform the same duties as an imam.

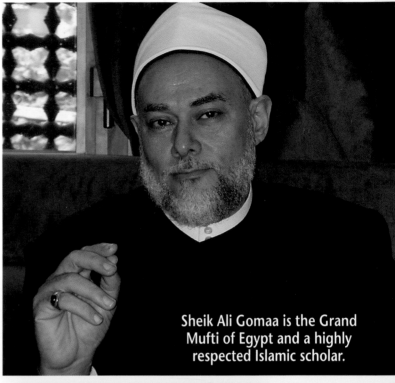

Sheik Ali Gomaa is the Grand Mufti of Egypt and a highly respected Islamic scholar.

The imam of the Grand Mosque of Mecca, Abdul Rahman bin Abdul Aziz al-Sudais, leads a congregation in prayer.

9

# Scriptures

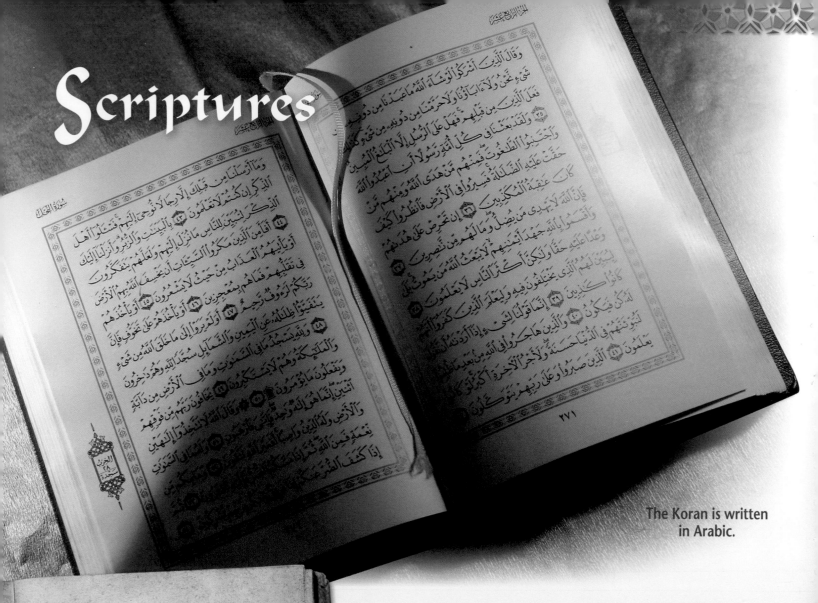

The Koran is written in Arabic.

To Allah belongs the kingdom of the Heavens and of the Earth, and all that is in them, and he is powerful over everything.

KORAN, SURAH 5:120

Create no mischief on Earth after it has been set in order.

KORAN, SURAH 7:56

The most important scripture for Muslims is the Koran. Muslims recite it every day and memorize as much of it as they can. Muslims also have great respect for another scripture called the Hadith.

## The Koran

The Koran tells Muslims how Allah wants them to live, so they will go to heaven when they die. It was revealed to the Prophet Mohammad by Allah through the angel Jibril.

The Koran is divided into 114 sections or chapters called surahs and is written in rhyming Arabic.

The Koran must be treated with great respect. Muslims always wash before they touch it and it must not be touched unnecessarily. It is usually put on a special table or a stand wrapped in cloth. No one is allowed to put anything on it, be noisy around it or eat while it is being read. When the Koran is not being read it is usually safely stored away.

## The Hadith

The Hadith is another important scripture to Muslims. It contains the sayings of Mohammad and explains the Koran, particularly the sections on law and religious observance. The Hadith also gives information about the Prophet Mohammad's life, such as how he prayed, his family, and the wars he fought in.

Mohammad passed on his teachings **orally** to his wives, family, and followers. They in turn told them to other people. The Hadith was first compiled as a text in the ninth century CE by two scholars called Bukhari and Muslim.

**Muslim women in Indonesia take part in a weekly reading of the scriptures.**

No man is a true believer unless he desires for his brother that which he desires for himself.

HADITH, MUSLIM
71–72

If you give charity openly it is well, and if you hide it and give it to the poor it is better for you.

HADITH, BUKHARI 2:271

And whoever is given knowledge is given indeed abundant wealth.

HADITH, BUKHARI 2:269

# Religious Leaders

The Prophet Mohammad is the most important religious leader to Muslims. After he died, his work was carried on by **caliphs**. An important caliph was Umar ibn al-Khattab.

## Mohammad 570–632 CE

Mohammad grew up in Mecca, Hijaz, which is now Saudi Arabia. He did not approve of the way his neighbors worshipped **idols**, got drunk and, Mohammad felt, treated women like slaves.

In 610 CE, the angel Jibril spoke to Mohammad: Jibril told him that he was to be Allah's last prophet. From that time until his death in 632 CE, Mohammad received regular messages from Allah. These teachings make up the Koran. Mohammad could not read and write but he memorized the teachings and they were written down later by his followers.

Not everybody appreciated Mohammad's teachings and he was forced to leave Mecca in 622 CE. Eight years later, with an army of 10 thousand men, he conquered Mecca with almost no resistance. Mohammad then forgave his enemies and the citizens became Muslims and worshipped Allah.

Mohammad was married to eight wives. He had three sons, who died young, and four daughters. He is buried in a tomb in the Mosque of the Prophet in Medina, Saudi Arabia.

For Muslims, the Sacred Mosque in Mecca is the holiest place on Earth.

Many Muslims visit the Mosque of the Prophet in Medina, Saudi Arabia, where the Prophet Mohammad and Umar ibn al-Khattab are buried.

## Umar ibn al-Khattab    584–644 CE

Umar ibn al-Khattab was the second caliph after Mohammad died. He ruled from 634 to 644 CE.

Umar was familiar with Mohammad and his teachings because his daughter was Mohammad's fourth wife. Umar was one of the leaders who helped collect and write down the Koran. He was worried that the people who recited the Koran could be killed in battle and the scripture would be lost.

There were many battles in Umar's lifetime. He conquered Palestine, Syria, Iraq, Egypt, Iran, North Africa, Armenia, and Persia, and spread Islam throughout these countries.

Umar administered the conquered lands without too much trouble. This was partly because the conquered people had not liked their previous rulers, particularly the Romans.

Umar was seen as a much fairer ruler. He kept some of the processes set up by the Romans and allowed non-Muslims with expertise to keep their roles in government. He issued a policy of tolerance toward Christians and Jews and did not force them to convert to Islam.

Not everybody appreciated Umar, however, and he was stabbed to death by a slave in 644 CE. As he was dying he appointed a committee to select the new caliph.

# Worship Practices

The most important worship practices for Muslims are praying five times a day and going on a pilgrimage to Mecca at least once in their lifetime.

## Praying

The Muslim word for prayer is salat. Muslims can pray anywhere, but it is considered best to pray at a mosque. Muslims must take their shoes off before entering a mosque and wash before they pray. This ritual washing is called wudu. It involves washing the hands and arms to the elbows, rinsing the mouth, nose and ears, wiping the hair, and washing the feet.

Muslims kneel on a mat and face in the direction of Mecca to pray. This is because Mecca is the religious center of the Muslim world.

### Prayer Times

Muslims practice salat every day of the week at set times. The five prayer times are:

☾ Fajr, which means dawn

☾ Dhuhr, which means midday

☾ Asr, which means afternoon

☾ Maghrib, which means sunset

☾ Isha, which means evening.

**This is the typical floor plan of a mosque.**

The five prayer times are for Muslims to remember Allah and seek his guidance, mercy, and forgiveness.

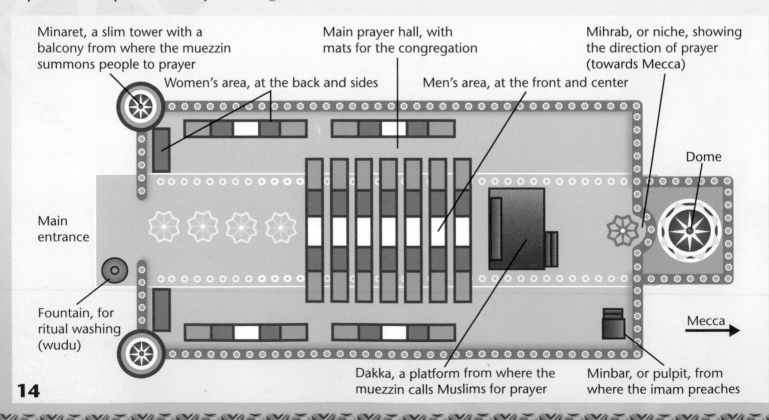

Minaret, a slim tower with a balcony from where the muezzin summons people to prayer

Women's area, at the back and sides

Main prayer hall, with mats for the congregation

Men's area, at the front and center

Mihrab, or niche, showing the direction of prayer (towards Mecca)

Dome

Main entrance

Fountain, for ritual washing (wudu)

Dakka, a platform from where the muezzin calls Muslims for prayer

Minbar, or pulpit, from where the imam preaches

Mecca

## Pilgrimage to Mecca

Muslims make the pilgrimage to Mecca during the month of Dhul-Hijja in the Islamic calendar. This pilgrimage is called the Hajj. Approximately 3 million people travel to Mecca at this time.

Some of the acts Muslims perform during the Hajj are:

☾ chanting prayers and walking around the Kaaba at least seven times in an anticlockwise direction

☾ drinking water from the Well of Zamzam

☾ visiting Mount Arafat

☾ visiting the Mount of Mercy, where Mohammad delivered his last sermon

☾ collecting pebbles at Muzdalifah

☾ going to the three stone pillars at the Village of Mina and throwing forty-nine pebbles at the pillar that represents Iblis. Iblis is the angel that makes trouble for Muslims.

### Ihram Clothing

When pilgrims reach Mecca they wear an ihram. This is two pieces of white cloth for men and a long dress for women, which leave only their faces and hands bare. This is to make everyone look similar, to symbolize that they are all equal in the sight of Allah.

Pilgrims circle the Kaaba, which is inside the Sacred Mosque in Mecca and is the holiest building in Islam.

Chinese Muslims celebrate the end of Ramadan with dancing.

# Festivals and Celebrations

Two celebrations that are extremely important to Muslims are Ramadan and Id al-fitr.

## Ramadan

Ramadan is the ninth month of the Muslim calendar. It is a special month as it was during Ramadan that the Koran was first revealed to the Prophet Mohammad. Each year, Ramadan begins eleven days earlier than in the previous year, so it is often observed in different seasons.

During Ramadan, Muslims aim to read all of the Koran. They also fast each day, from dawn to sunset, unless they are young children, are ill, or are travelling. Money saved by missing a meal is given to the poor before the end of Ramadan. This is so the poor can buy food and new clothes in time for Id al-fitr, the feast that marks the end of Ramadan.

Muslims say fasting brings them closer to Allah and reminds them about the poor and the hungry. The Koran also says fasting teaches self-control.

## Id al-fitr

Id al-fitr is the feast that follows Ramadan. It is a time of much rejoicing and everyone wears new clothes to celebrate. Id ad-fitr is announced by:

☾ the call to prayer from the mosque

☾ gun fire

☾ an announcement on radio or television.

Once Id al-fitr is announced, everyone cries "Id Mubarak," meaning "Happy Id," and people exchange hugs and handshakes. Then everyone goes to the mosque for special prayers and a sermon. The service is about half an hour long.

After attending the mosque, families break their fast by eating dates. They then pray together and have a celebration feast. This is followed by a three- or four-day holiday.

**Pakistani Muslim women wear colorful new clothes for Id al-fitr.**

The Islamic calendar is different from the Western **Gregorian calendar**. Holy days fall on the same date each Islamic year but over time they will occur in different seasons. Here are some of the major Islamic holy days, with the approximate Gregorian months in which they will occur:

**Islamic New Year**
January

**Day of Ashura**
Muharram 10
January or February

**Milad un Nabi (Mohammad's Birthday)**
Rabiul Awal 12 or 17
March or April

**Ramadan**
The whole month of Ramadan
August or September

**Id al-fitr**
Shawwal 1 to 3
September or October

**The Hajj (pilgrimage to Mecca)**
Dhul-Hijja 8 to 13
November or December

# Important Muslims

Important Muslims include the women in Mohammad's family and the ancient Muslim astronomers and mathematicians. Astronomy helped Muslims determine the times for prayer, the date of the new moon, and the precise direction of Mecca.

## Khadijah Bint Khuwaylid    560–620 CE

Mohammad's first wife, Khadijah Bint Khuwaylid, was a successful businesswoman. She supported Mohammad so he could spend his time worshipping Allah and teaching people about Islam. Khadijah encouraged Mohammad, comforted him, and believed in him. Muslims see her as a good role model for Muslim women.

## A'isha Bint AbuBakar    613–678 CE

A'isha Bint AbuBakar was Mohammad's third wife. She is remembered for her work recording and preserving the Hadith. A'isha was known for her skills in mathematics, poetry, and medicine, and for her passion for educating women and children. Scholars still study her teachings today.

## Fatima Al Zahra 615–632 CE

Fatima Al Zahra was Mohammad and Khadijah's youngest daughter. She was known for her courage because she often had to defend her father's teachings. She was also known for her generosity. Fatima gave away so many of her possessions that she often had very little for herself. A center for women's rights in Baghdad, Iraq, was named after her.

Women learn computer skills at the Fatima Al Zahra Center for Women's Rights in Baghdad, Iraq.

### Nasir al-Din al-Tusi
### 1201–1274 CE

Nasir al-Din al-Tusi was in charge of one of the world's first astronomical observatories, which was built in northwest Iran in the 1200s. The scientists used instruments called astrolabes to study the sky. Nasir was a very clever man. He observed the movements of the planets and wrote about trigonometry, geometry, biology, and ethics.

### Mohammad ibn Musa al-Khwarazmi
### 780–850 CE

Mohammad ibn Musa al-Khwarazmi lived in what is now Iraq. He worked at an academy called the House of Wisdom in Baghdad, and wrote books on algebra, astronomy, and Arabic numbers. He came up with the word "Al-jabr" to describe the type of math now known the world over as "algebra."

### Ibn al-Haytham     965–1040 CE

Ibn al-Haytham was born in Basra, Iraq, in 965 CE. He was an astronomer who worked out that the Milky Way is made up of many stars that are a long way from Earth.

Astronomers Nasir, Mohammad, and Ibn are depicted on Iranian and Iraqi stamps and money.

Kafias are mostly worn by men in the Middle East.

# Clothes and Food

The Koran has specific teachings about clothes and food. Muslims believe that following these teachings is the proper way to behave.

## Clothes for Muslim Men

Muslim men often wear a long gown or a long-sleeved top over baggy pants. They may also wear a kufi, which is a short, crocheted cap. In the **Middle East**, Muslim men may wear a head-covering called a kafia. It touches the shoulders and is held in position by a band around the forehead. Kafias help to protect the men from the sun and sand.

## Clothes for Muslim Women

The Koran advises Muslim women to dress modestly. This is to prevent men from being tempted by female beauty. Some Muslim women wear a hijab when they are out in public. A hijab is a scarf-like garment worn over the head. In Iran, Saudi Arabia, and Afghanistan, Muslim women wear a garment called a chador, which covers them from head to toe so that only their eyes can be seen.

Women who wear a hijab or chador do not have to wear them at home. Most Turkish Muslim women do not wear a hijab as the government does not allow it.

Chadors are loose-fitting in order to hide the female form.

Live sheep are shipped to the Middle East, where they are ritually slaughtered in the halal method.

## Food

The Koran has several rules about food Muslims can and cannot eat. Food that is "haram" is forbidden by Islamic law. Food that is "halal" is allowed.

### Haram Food

It is forbidden for Muslims to eat any of the following:
☾ animals that are not killed in the halal method
☾ pork (or any type of pig meat)
☾ blood
☾ meat that has been offered to idols, because the animal was slaughtered without the name of Allah being said.

It is also considered haram to drink alcohol.

### Halal Food

Sunni Muslims consider all fish to be halal, or allowed to be eaten. Shi'ite Muslims consider only some kinds of fish to be halal.

For meat to be halal, the animal must be ritually slaughtered. The correct method is to cut the throat so the blood drains quickly from the animal's body. This is so the animal does not suffer and does not realize it is going to die.

Muslims must begin their meals by saying the **basmala**. They say, "In the name of Allah the Compassionate, the Caring."

# Birth

When Muslim babies are born, the first words they hear are very important. The naming ceremony of a Muslim baby is also important.

### First Words a Baby Hears

When a baby is born, the parents recite the *Adhan*, or call to prayer, into the baby's right ear. Then the parents whisper the *Iqamah*, or the call to stand up for the ritual prayer, into the baby's left ear.

ADHAN

Allah is most great
Allah is most great
I testify that there is no god but Allah
I testify that there is no god but Allah
I testify that Mohammad is
    the Messenger of Allah
Come to prayer
Come to salvation
Allah is great
There is no god but Allah.

IQAMAH

Allah is most great
I testify that there is no god but Allah
I bear witness that Mohammad is
    the Messenger of Allah
Come to prayer
Come to salvation
Prayer is ready
Prayer is ready
Allah is Great
Allah is Great
There is no god except Allah.

## Naming Ceremony

Seven days after a Muslim baby is born, a naming ceremony is held for them. The baby's head is shaved and the hair is weighed. The parents donate the weight in silver to the poor.

Suitable names for Muslim children include Mohammad or any of the names of his family. Names that show a close relationship to Allah are also suitable, such as the boy's name Abdullah, which means "servant of Allah."

### Male Muslim Babies

Male Muslim babies are also **circumcised** during the naming ceremony. In some Muslim countries parents delay the time the boy is circumcised. In Java and Yemen, boys are circumcised when they are ten to twelve years old.

In India, Muslim parents take their baby to a mosque to pray before the circumcision is performed.

23

Muslim girls are taught to look after the home in preparation for marriage.

# Growing Up

Muslim children are taught household chores as they grow up, to help make them responsible adults. There are also two significant stages of growing up. These are the age of distinguishing and the age of maturity.

## Learning to Be Responsible

When Muslim children become teenagers, their parents begin to teach them household chores and encourage them to share family responsibilities. Young women are taught how to take care of the house and cook. Young men are taught how to do repairs. This is to prepare them for marriage or if their parents die young.

Muslims often marry when they are still teenagers. The Koran and the Hadith both encourage young marriage.

## Age of Distinguishing

Mothers who are divorced may keep their children at home until they have reached the age of distinguishing. For a boy, this is when they are about seven years old. This is considered the time when he is old enough to dress, clean, and feed himself independently. Girls can stay with their mother until they are nine so they can learn more about female habits and duties.

## Age of Maturity

The age of maturity is when a Muslim child is considered an adult. There is no fixed age but it is usually at 15 years, unless the child shows signs of physical and sexual development before then.

A POEM FOR MY TEENAGERS

In happy times, praise Allah
In difficult moments, seek Allah
In quiet times, worship Allah
In painful moments, trust Allah
And in every moment, thank Allah

KAWKAB JEDA

Boys who reach the age of maturity often attend classes in their local mosque.

# Marriage

Islamic marriages follow the teachings of the Koran. They are not always based on romantic love, but on ancestry, property, how religious the partner is, and the benefits to both families. The Koran allows husbands to have up to four wives as long as he can support them financially and fairly.

## Preparation for the Wedding

The groom must give his future bride a **mahr** before they marry. This is usually money or jewelry, which is hers to keep and use as she wants. Muslim women keep their own surname when they get married.

In Tanzania, the bride has henna-painted hands and the groom wears a head covering.

## Wedding Clothes

The clothes a Muslim bride or groom wears depends on the country in which they live. In India the bride will wear a sari and have her hands painted with **henna**. If a Muslim couple marries in a Western country, such as the United States or Canada, a bride will normally wear a white dress and veil.

## Wedding Ceremony

The Muslim wedding ceremony is very simple. The local imam usually performs the ceremony. He reads from the Koran and then gives a short talk about marriage and the couple's responsibilities to each other. The couple then declares their acceptance of each other and the imam declares that they are husband and wife. The imam then asks the congregation to recite the Koran.

The most important part of the ceremony, however, is the signing of the marriage contract. Once the contract is signed, the bride and groom are officially married.

After the ceremony the guests say "baarakallahu lakum wa baraka alaikum," which means "may Allah bless you and invoke his benediction on you." The wedding ceremony usually ends with a feast.

After the wedding ceremony, friends and family celebrate with a wedding feast.

# Death and the Afterlife

Pallbearers carry the body from the mosque to the cemetery.

Muslims follow a number of rituals when someone is dying and at the funeral. They also believe in life after death.

## The Last Hours

If a Muslim is still conscious when he or she is dying, he or she will ask family and friends for forgiveness and blessings and to read from the Koran. A Muslim wants the last word heard before dying to be "Allah."

## The Funeral

After a Muslim dies, his or her body is washed all over with soap by someone of the same sex, either at home, at the mosque, or at a special Muslim building.

The body is wrapped in a **shroud** made of white cloth. Women are wrapped in five layers of cloth and men three. The body is then taken to an open space or the mosque for funeral prayers. The funeral is led by an imam or by a family member, with a short speech by the imam.

### The Burial

After the funeral, the body is physically carried to the cemetery. This is considered more respectful than riding in a comfortable car. Muslims do not use coffins unless they have to for health reasons. The face of the body is turned to the right and the body is buried so that the person faces Mecca. Muslims do not believe in cremation.

## Life After Death

Muslims believe in heaven and hell, and where they go depends on their deeds. Fortunately, in Islam, good deeds count ten times more than bad deeds. Muslims believe there are seven levels of hell, with **hypocrites** being put on the lowest level.

Muslims do not go to heaven or hell straight after they die. Their **soul** waits in barzakh, which is the waiting place until Judgment Day when Allah judges everybody.

Prayer and the pilgrimage to Mecca are considered good deeds which will help a Muslim get to heaven, or paradise.

# Islam Around the World

Islam is the second largest religion in the world, with approximately 1.5 billion followers. Muslims can be found all over the world, with many living in Egypt, Iran, Iraq, Jordan, Syria, Algeria, Libya, Morocco, Tunisia, Somalia, Sudan, Bangladesh, India, Pakistan, Russia, China, Europe, Lebanon, and Turkey.

The country with the world's largest Muslim community is Indonesia. It has 202 million Muslims, which make up 86 percent of the population.

**This map shows the top thirteen Muslim countries.**

ARCTIC OCEAN

ARCTIC OCEAN

**TURKEY**
99 percent

**TUNISIA**
98 percent

**IRAN**
98 percent

**MOROCCO**
99 percent

**AFGHANISTAN**
99 percent

ATLANTIC OCEAN

**SAUDI ARABIA**
100 percent

PACIFIC OCEAN

**ALGERIA**
99 percent

**YEMEN**
100 percent

PACIFIC OCEAN

**INDONESIA**
86 percent

**MAURITANIA**
100 percent

**MALDIVES**
100 percent

**COMOROS**
98 percent

**SOMALIA**
100 percent

INDIAN OCEAN

**KEY**

| | |
|---|---|
| | area of country |
| **IRAN** | name of country |
| **95 percent** | percentage of country population that is Muslim |

SOUTHERN OCEAN

SOUTHERN OCEAN

# Glossary

| | |
|---|---|
| basmala | the first verse of the first Surah of the Koran |
| caliphs | leaders of Muslim nations |
| circumcised | having the foreskin removed from the penis |
| congregations | groups of people meeting to worship Allah |
| fasting | not eating, or eating very little |
| Gregorian calendar | the most widely used calendar in the world, based on the cycle of the Sun |
| henna | a reddish dye made from the leaves of the henna plant |
| hypocrites | people who pretend to believe in something to hide their real beliefs |
| idols | images used as objects of worship |
| Kaaba | the most sacred shrine in Islam, located in Mecca and said to contain a rock from the altar built by the prophet Abraham |
| Last Prophet | the last person through whom Allah speaks, after which there will be no other |
| mahr | a gift, often of money, that a Muslim man must give to his wife and can never ask for back |
| Mecca | the home of Islam |
| Middle East | the area around the eastern Mediterranean, from Turkey to northern Africa and east to Iran |
| orally | spoken, rather than written |
| pilgrimage | a journey, usually a long one, made to a sacred place |
| Ramadan | the ninth month in the Muslim calendar |
| scriptures | sacred writings |
| sermons | speeches that explain sections of the Koran and advise followers how to use the teachings in their daily lives |
| shroud | a cloth that is wrapped around a body before it is buried |
| soul | a person's spirit, which lives forever |
| submits | accepts without arguing |
| successors | the people who follow (in order) |

# Index